FROM
TRAUMA TO PEACE
OUR JOURNEY

BY
DR. BRIDGETTE HEARD

ISBNs

Paperback: 979-8-9857486-0-4

eBook : 979-8-9857486-1-1

Dedications

To My Husband, Eric Heard:

We are forever one in our love for each other and our children.

To Our Children:

This book is dedicated to each of you:

Haley Lorene, Bria Leigh, and Eric Lincoln

All of you are my heartbeats. I am so thankful that God has allowed your father and I to become your parents. Words cannot adequately express our love for each of you.

Also, To:

My Parents (Reverend Larry and Joanne) and Sisters (Dr. Adrienne, MD, and Alesha, MA):

Thank you for giving my sisters and me the confidence to reach for the stars in all that we do, while keeping God number one in our lives.

Your continued support and love have been a staple in my life for which I am forever grateful.

Eric's parents (The Late Tommy Head and Leora):

Thank you for providing the support Eric needed during the most difficult times of our lives.

The Williams, Howard, & Heard/Cason Families:

What can I say?

"We will ALWAYS be there for one another!"

I could not have asked for a better family.

Acknowledgments

I want to thank all of those who have supported and nurtured me throughout my life.

To my grandparents, who are no longer here on this side of heaven, I love and miss you. You will always be a part of my healing as I remember the love, prayers, and teachings provided to me as a child.

Thank you to my pastors and their wives from Decatur, Illinois (Rev. Dr. CD Stuart; Gladys) and Peoria, Illinois, (Rev. Deveraux Hubbard; Kristie) who have helped me grow spiritually. My spiritual growth has allowed me to handle difficult circumstances through my faith and dependence on God.

Tea Roses to My Line Sisters of S.S.MANIFEST, all of my Gamma Sorors, & my Sorors of Nu Pi Omega.

We help each for, for we know there's no other...like our sisterhood.

Table of Contents

What Others Are Saying About From Trauma to Peace – Our Journey:

The significance of the book for me, was watching God change the circumstances based upon His promises. In the book of Psalm 103, we learn that God's mercy is far-reaching- even beyond our finite knowledge. The bible teaches us to depend on God, in all situations.

—Reverend Larry Williams
(Father of Bridgette Heard, Grandfather of Haley, Bria, and Eric)

Dr. Bridgette Heard wrote *From Trauma to Peace* to teach others that even the smallest amount of hope and faith can make a big difference. This book is a must read for anyone on a journey relating to trauma. This book does a great job of highlighting a Mother's Love and God's Peace. This book is a "must-read," and ends with a powerful call to action that will inspire every reader.

— Jennifer Strickland,
Mother, Overcomer, Believer & Marketing Manager

We all need to understand how to make mental mind shifts that allow us to live in peace. This book provides a detailed account of two pivotal events that led to healing. This healing would have occurred regardless of the outcome and that's one of the most significant parts. It's about healing from the inside out, regardless of the outcome.

—**Donna Crowder,**
Mother, School Teacher, Youth Advocate, Philanthropist

The Williams family has experienced many traumatic events. Though those events have brought us closer together, the experiences were really hard to go through. *Trauma to Peace* is a great book that provides a look into what our family experienced in 2020, but even more than that, it shows what anyone can put into practice how to go from trauma to peace in a sustainable way.

—**Danita Williams**
Mother, Grandmother

Wow!! Thank you, Dr. Bridgette, for choosing to be completely vulnerable in sharing your spiritual journey of God bringing you and your family from several tests to a testimony. A woman strong in faith, delivered from her breaking point to find joy and peace again is a victory worth celebrating. An inspiring read!!

—**Sheila Gordon,**

Greater Purpose Consulting, President and Principal Advisor

This is a necessary read, written by an amazing woman of God! This book is set to change your mindset with refreshing new concepts and ways to strategically set your personal goals and accomplishment! Dr. Bridgette Heard gives you all of the tools needed to discover your true self. Get ready to transform your life!

—Adrienne Jones-Yarbrough
Mother and Owner of A Sharp Effect Salon

Epilogue

Eric and I have been married for almost 26 years now. Our oldest daughter, Haley is turning 24 soon; Bria, our middle child is turning 23 (nine days before Haley turns 24); and our youngest, Eric, just turned 19 a few months ago. Our family has been through varying degrees of trials and tribulations. For years, I wondered why God allowed us to experience what I considered "so much pain." We seemed to be pain magnets. As I learned to tune my heart towards the love God truly has for me and my family, I went from "why us" to "why not us?"

It is such a blessing knowing that God can use us to spread the good news. Regardless of our circumstances, He is present and everything we know Him to be. He is loving, kind, protective, all-powerful, everywhere, comforting…. God Is!! He is everything that we have needed Him to be in our happiest and our saddest moments in life. To know that He sees and feels our pain is just one testament to WHO he is. He does not cause us pain to hurt us but to foster our growth.

Just think about this – If we never experienced pain, how would we know and truly believe in what God could do on our behalf? Pain hurts. Trauma is real – but none of it is permanent if you can change your mindset and see the event from the lens of God.

As a family, we were not only traumatized by the circumstances that surrounded the birth of our son but also the hurt that befell him - our daughters' little brother. We were also in total disbelief that we could go from a happy place to the darkest place we had ever experienced all within the matter of one hour. Believe me, it is not a competition to see who can make it to the other side and find peace in the midst of trauma. It is a journey. The journey that God allows us to go through changes who we are and how we think.

Everyone's journey may be different, but it is rarely short. At times while yearning to find any good during our pain, we question the Word of God. *How can all things work for the good if we are called until His will?* I had to learn that the second part of that last statement is the most important part. *Called to his will*, for me, means we are a part of His overall purpose to make us into who and what we need to be to help a world that has yet to truly know the splendor of His love for us.

I have learned that making it through the journey of life – going from trauma to peace is 90% mindset and 10% strategy. Yes, there is a strategy, but your mind has to be ready to receive – thus 90% is mindset. While mindset seems like an abstract construct, I argue that is defined clearly by what we choose to believe and follow, based on what we know or have been taught.

I have added an overview of a portion of the journey we were on in December of 2020. Notice that I stated "a portion of our journey." We were already on the journey, dealing with other life issues, then shocked by the event that made us want to turn back, but we knew that the only way was forward – regardless of the outcome. We were still being tested.

It is in this critical moment that deciding to remain on the journey with the faith we will come out on the other side in a better state was important. When you are hurt to your emotional core, your faith can waver or it can become stronger, but we have to make a choice if fear or faith will rule our lives during that season.

Foreword

When I think of the word peace, *I hear sounds* – the sounds of an ocean, the sounds of the wind rustling through the leaves in the trees. When I think of peace, *I see images of love* – the love from my husband, children, parents, sisters, extended family members, and a few close friends. When I think of peace, *I feel hugs.* I feel the hugs of my grandmothers when I would visit them. When I think of peace, *I smell the scent* of fresh flowers when walking through botanical gardens.

Peace is so joyful, that when I close my eyes and extend my arms, I can touch it. Peace is what many long for in life. Peace encompasses all that allows us to feel a different connection to that which we love and those things that make us feel comfortable.

On the other end of the spectrum is hurt. Throughout this book, I refer to hurt in terms of trauma. When I think of trauma, I think of an emotional, psychological, and physical pain that is describable only by those who experience it. The journey they are on looks different, based on the circumstance. The journey that one encounters upon experiencing trauma is connected to their past, present, and possibly their future.

Instead of the calming sounds and feelings of peace, experiencing trauma is very different. In trauma, there is often a deafening silence or loud commotion that clouds the mind and many times, makes it nearly impossible to focus and think clearly. Instead of seeing the love and feeling hugs, some feel nothing positive as shock sets in and emotions are blocked by fear and anxiety. That which we hope to touch seems, and is often, untouchable. Feeling empty or the fullness of feeling sad can overtake those who experience trauma and can lead to desperation and the lack of resolution and calm – all of which can lead to darkness.

The definitions provided, I consider to be operational, though to some, they may not show the complexity some like to provide when defining the concepts, I address herein. I want the definitions provided to be simple, applicable, and relatable for those who are or have experienced trauma.

The purpose of this book is to identify my encounters with both trauma and peace, as a mother, while providing an overview of what I watched my other family members experience.

The resolutions that I discovered on my journey may not be the same for you, but they are what worked for me. The journey from trauma to peace is one that did not occur quickly for me. My journey seemed like a marathon, not a sprint. I experienced setbacks. I experienced isolation. I encountered thoughts that I could not share with family or friends. I found myself in mental valleys of desperation which led to feelings of hopelessness, ultimately delaying me from reaching the mountaintop where peace resides.

My journey included three major parts: valleys, hills, and the mountaintop. The peace for me was found at the mountaintop. I had to learn the lessons in the valley and hill moments, and I often found myself slipping from the hill back down into the valley. These emotional metaphors were as real in my mind as reaching out and touching something tangible. They were real experiences that began in my mind, fed my heart, came out of my mouth, and led to many actions that have either hindered or helped to further my progress towards peace.

The most important part of it all is that I learned that making it through this treacherous journey leads to peace, which ultimately means victory. There are different ways to get through the journey, but there is always a way to make it to complete peace.

I pray that however you get to the other side, you pick up the lessons along the way that will allow you to experience peace. Once you can navigate through the journey and experience true peace, never forget what it took to make it through the journey. If you remember that you were truly never alone, it will help you when going through the next life event.

Preface

From Trauma to Peace discusses the events surrounding several personal traumas. These events have changed the fiber of my being. I am a different person because of these experiences. I see and have a clear connection to the evolution of my thoughts – spanning over my 49 years of life. I now understand the purpose of the trauma, which allows me to see the journey that prepared me for today.

I have experienced several events in my life which would be classified as trauma, but for the purpose of this book, I will discuss the latest one in the most detail. This most recent event is central to my overall purpose of helping others to transform their thinking and way of life. The first event, which occurred 18 years ago, happened to *me*, although my son was involved indirectly. The second event, which directly involved my son, occurred less than a year ago today, on December 18, 2020, around 7:30 p.m. I went from being a patient to being an observer. Experiencing both positions allowed me to observe cataclysmic circumstances that has now led to my transformed life.

What God had in store for my life, for my child's life, and my family's, allowed me to see things from the vantage point of a mother. The pain of trauma is crippling. In that hurt, I learned that sometimes it takes mental pain to get our attention. Sometimes the ground underneath our feet must shake and frighten us to help focus us on what we need to gain. While in and working through the trauma, we may feel like we are in the middle of quicksand, and no one knows we are there. That is when we need to yell for help and scream out, "I'm stuck!" Even though I felt as though I was sinking, deep inside, I knew God was there and that was truly enough. At the time, it did not feel like that was enough, because I did not want to travel through the journey. I wanted resolution right away, as many of us do. The reality is that God's timing is always right. It is perfect. His timely provides the grace we need to see Him as the Great I Am, that He is.

The other side of the areas where we are stuck is where we become determined to take our negative thoughts captive and lean on what we know is true. Some may think about the sermons and bible scriptures we listened to and read over the years. For others, we must remember experiences we have endured or known others to have endured and successfully made it through. Looking at the situation or event from a different perspective does not mean we forget what happened. It does not mean we are over it. It does mean, however, that we can see the details and outcome of the event differently. We can now see from a lens that we did not have access to while we were stuck. Once we change how we think, we can change how we react.

I learned that trauma was planted in my life to set me free from negative thinking and to help others as well. Now, to most, that might sound like an oxymoron, but as you read the details of the two specific events that happened, I will unfold the trepidation I had and how it contributed to me experiencing freedom.

Chapter 1

Our Family Grows Along with Heartache

On May 23, 2000, my god-sister, first cousin, and best friend Yolanda passed away. She had given birth to twin boys three months prior to the unexpected death. She was twenty-eight years old. Jesus decided to take her back, leaving five beautiful children on this earth without a mother. Though this was not the first traumatic event I had experienced, it was the first one that was so impactful, I remained on the journey to peace for a long time thereafter. In my mind, it did not make sense that God would allow that to occur. I was not spiritually mature enough to understand the situation from the vantage point of the Lord.

I could not see that the truth of God's strength being perfect in the midst of pain. It felt like every time something good happened, something bad followed. Many may feel this way, but know it is a part of a process (journey) that we go through. It can do one of two things – make us stronger or keep us from growing. The irony is that we have to decide how we will allow our circumstances /traumatic events impact our lives.

Within a year of Yolanda's death, my husband and I experienced a miscarriage. God decided to take our child when I was fourteen weeks pregnant. It was shocking and hurtful because my husband and I were able to see our child's heartbeat and see the budding of his/her arms and legs.

After outpatient surgery, our baby was removed from my womb. I knew life had to continue and that I had joined many women that experienced a miscarriage as well. I focused on being present for the two children we were blessed to have, yet always prayed for and called my third child *my angel.*

I recall my discussion with God as I wept over the miscarriage. I wondered if I had done something to upset God. I told God, "I want to know you better. I want to be closer to you. I need you." Let me give you a quick reality check about that prayer. When I asked God to know Him better, I had no idea His methods of making that become a reality. We should all desire to know God better but understand this: His ways are not our ways. You may not experience what my family experienced – you may experience something less traumatic or more traumatic. If you are serious about knowing God in such a way that your mindset shifts to where you attempt to see things and people the way God does, you may get the gift of suffering that I received.

Yes, I call it a gift, because now that I have a real relationship with God, I will never be who I was again. I have a renewed mind. He taught me and stayed with me through my journey of hurt. I have a peace that I refuse to give away when things go wrong. I have been tested repeatedly, and sometimes I get it right. Sometimes I get it wrong, but God embraces me and reassures me every time that He has me and my family in the palm of his hands.

A few other hurtful situations occurred after that. It felt like a very long time before life was "normal" again, but as I rounded that next corner in life, our family began to metaphorically see the sun through the clouds. At this point, I still lacked the mental faculties that I have since developed, but I felt better as we entered 2002 to find out I was pregnant again.

In August 2002, our first and only son was born. My husband and I had two daughters and we were having a boy. Haley was four years old and Bria was three years old at the time of Eric's birth. I had what older generations call "stair-step children" –multiple births within a short time span. Our daughters are fewer than twelve months apart, which raised many eyebrows as when we attended church. I thought it was great to have children so close in age. I always considered them my twin girls.

During my pregnancy with our son, I had a few complications. I wore a heart monitor for several months as my heart raced. I did not care what I had to endure; I was just excited to have a boy. Immediately after the heart monitor was removed, I found out my pregnancy was considered high risk. And so the next journey began.

In this picture, I was seven months pregnant.
Yes, I had two full months to go.

My son's bladder was enlarged. As many know, while the baby is in uterus, the amniotic fluid is made up partly of sterile urine from the child. Because my son's bladder was enlarged, he urinated a lot, which caused my stomach to look like I was having twins. Initially, the doctor considered inducing labor before my son's actual due date but decided to refer me to a specialist. Besides a very large stomach, I was fine. My baby was fine. I could barely feel him move the entire pregnancy because of the extra fluid. I would often do what many mothers do while pregnant. I would push one side of my stomach to make him kick or flip. My baby always complied. He would give me such a kick, I would literally laugh out loud and tell him, "Okay, okay, I'm sorry! I was just checking on you!"

On August 27, 2002, our son was born. My husband and I prayed for a boy after having two girls, and God granted our request. We named our Eric. The night he was born, his heart rate started to drop, so my doctor decided that I needed a C-section. This was my first C-section and I was terrified. Only my husband was allowed join me in the operating room.

They gave my husband the blue scrub-like outfit he needed to place over his clothes and the paper booties to cover his shoes. They told him he needed to hurry. My son was fighting to make his entrance into the world, but he could not come the way he was trying to enter.

They prepped me while my husband was rushed into the operating room. I remember the doctor telling me, "Here we go." After a minute or so, I heard my baby crying. Oh, the joy of hearing that sound. My husband looked at our son and said, "We have a son!" and kissed me. Our baby was wrapped and handed to my husband who put our son to my face so I could kiss him.

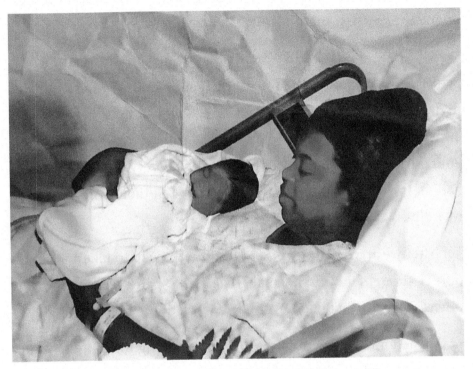

August, 2020 – Eric's first day in the world.

Within the next thirty minutes or so, I began to feel weak and told the doctor that something was wrong. I could feel a tingling that went from my toes and rose throughout my body until my teeth began to chatter. I was freezing. We were told that a lot of blood was lost during the C-section but that I would be okay.

We believed him.

Instead of the normal 48 hours allowed by insurance companies for new mothers and babies to remain in the hospital, I stayed five days. The incision was painful, I was weak. I could not hold my baby for more than a minute or so. The nurse helped me breastfeed him because the energy that I expected to have was not there.

My son and I were discharged from the hospital. I was prescribed pain pills to help with the pain from my incision. Prior to driving back to where we lived, which was about ninety minutes away, we had to stop by my parents' home to get our daughters. The entire drive to their home was excruciating. Every time my husband had to make a stop, turn, drive over a pothole, the pain was relentless.

After we arrived at my parents' home, I began to take a few pain pills. I thought it was normal to feel this pain. I did not know otherwise, because I had never had a C-section.

We left after a few hours. My dad was going to bring my mom later that night so she could stay with me for a few weeks to help while my husband went back to work.

As we traveled home, I felt the tingling in my feet again. The feeling began to go up my legs, my chest, arms, and my teeth started to chatter. My husband turned the heat on. He stopped at a gas station at my request and bought a soda for me. I took a few more pain pills. The pills helped for several hours. Within a few hours, I had taken four pills, which was not how it was prescribed, but I was out of options to temper the pain.

A few hours after arriving home, my parents arrived, and my husband left for work. My mom held my baby as the girls played. I laid on the couch in our family room. After some time passed, I told my mother I was hot, then cold, then hot again. She called my oldest sister, who is a physician. She told my mom to take my temperature. I had a fever, yet the chills kept coming – now I was experiencing chills every hour. I could not eat.

My sister told my mom to call my doctor, then to call my husband.

My doctor instructed my mom to get me to the hospital and my husband rushed home. I told my mom that I would be right back. I bought several cans of formula prior to going to Peoria to give birth to our son. I told her that if I was not back and the baby was hungry, she could just give him the formula.

I had no idea that I would not be able to hold and kiss my children for the next nine weeks. I was in critical condition and placed in the intensive care unit on a respirator – breathing for me most of the time at 100%. I was diagnosed with E. coli. We were told that disease was in my bloodstream. When my stomach was cut for the C-Section, the air hit my blood and the bacteria began to spread very quickly.

I do not know how I got it, but it wreaked havoc on my heart, kidneys, lungs, and brain function. After my release from the ICU, I stayed in the hospital for rehabilitation for a few more weeks before our insurance company agent stated that I had to either be placed in a rehabilitation facility or receive in home physical and occupational therapy. I had to relearn how to walk and talk. Learning to talk was the hardest thing for me because I could not speak to my children. They did not care that I was in a wheelchair. They wanted me to talk.

I remember the joy of holding my son again. I just looked at him and smiled. My girls jumped on the couch to hug me. They were talking so much and I absolutely loved it. I could only talk in a very low whisper. My girls would say "Huh? Mommy we can't hear you!" What they did not know was that my greatest joy was to hear my girls talk and my son make sounds.

The Lesson I Learned: If you can find some understanding in the trauma, you will begin to feel God's presence. Sometimes you do not get *why* it happened, but you will know as you grow closer to God that it was a part of a master plan.

The journey in 2002 was about how God showed His omnipotence by baffling the physicians with the complexity of my illness. It detailed the effectiveness of the fervent prayers my mother, grandmothers, and other loved ones sent to God on my behalf. It was about showing the importance of faith and having confidence in someone so powerful, He could even cause the bacteria to be eradicated. It was to show that when the doctors did not know what to do, God stepped in so that I remained on the side of the living because my assignment was not yet completed.

Chapter 2

Seeing Trauma from a Different Vantage Point

A Drunk Driver Almost Killed My Son - 18 Years Later

Eighteen years later in 2021, our family encountered trauma again. It is much harder for me to write this, because it involved my child, my son. It involved the son whom I almost lost to miscarriage during pregnancy. It involved the son I was carrying when I contracted E. coli and almost lost my own life. It seemed strange at first, but as I reflect, I understand that it was a story of going through something devastating and coming out on the other side of it. Not having all of the details as to *why* it happened, but understanding that *it needed to happen* for me to be in the place that I'm in right now - a place of peace, a place of gratefulness.

When I looked at the pictures of the car after the collision almost a year later, I knew that anyone who was in the car should not have survived. There was no physical space for two people to fit inside the car without being crushed to death.

An observer sees objects like a wrecked car and often makes generalizations based on logic. Logic tells us that something looks like an impossibility based on what we believe to be true. Logic appears to be reasonable as we observe from the outside looking in based on our perceptions of the order and severity of that which caused the situation.

13

If I had looked at the pictures taken by the newspaper or onlookers, I do not know if I would have been able to pray and believe restoration was possible. Our thought processes can impact how we make decisions. Our thoughts have a lot of power. If those images had entered my mind, my son may not be alive today. I would not have been able to open my soul in prayer before the Lord. I would have doubted, at that time, that it was possible for my son to have survived such a horrific accident.

Our society has learned to think its way into what they believe is real and what they believe is unreal. We can see it in politics, for example. Based on what news channel you watch, there might be a slight slant as policies or politicians are discussed. When we look at belief systems, it is based on perceptions of how political parties will support those things we believe to be right in our own minds. Some of this comes from our subconscious – which is fed from our environments in which we grew up in, were surrounded by, taught to believe, and the like. Those subconscious thoughts become conscious when we hear political candidates talk about issues that we have learned to believe as good or bad.

Once our subconscious reminds us that something is bad based on experiences and/or situations, our conscious minds believe it wholeheartedly. Once we believe in our hearts, we speak those things into the universe. When we speak those things, they become true, even if only to us.

The following pictures show the Camry when it was new and within a few hours after it was hit with my son and his friend in it after being hit by a 25-year-old drunk driver. The picture to the right is the end of the crash site. My son and his friend were trapped in a parked car from behind. The car slid and was stopped by the electric pole that you see in the picture.

This is my son's car before the crash

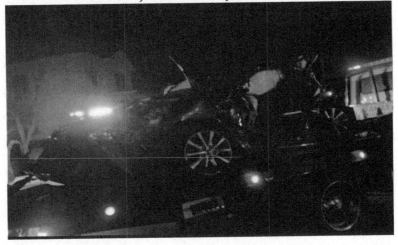

This is my son's car after the crash.

This is my son's car once it was in the tow yard. My husband and oldest daughter Haley retrieved some items from the car before it was crushed. To see a picture of the car in the daylight was absolutely devastating.

Chapter 3

December 18, 2020: A Day I Will Never Forget

*D*ecember 18th was cold and windy. Winter was officially here. This was the time of year when I loved to bake cookies and pies while watching Christmas movies. This was the one of my favorite times of the year for many reasons. It is a time when the cares of the world were a little less intense because everyone seemed happy.

For the first time, my husband, children, parents, sisters, niece, nephew and I had planned to spend Christmas in a large cabin in Missouri. Although as a family we spend every Christmas together, this year was going to be different. We were not going to get together at one of our homes, make Christmas breakfast, and take multiple trips trudging through the snow bringing in gifts. This year, we were scheduled to stay several days and nights in a home together, making Christmas cookies and pies together and watching Christmas movies.

My husband and I had already gotten our COVID tests and negative results. As the day went on, our daughters and son finally decided to leave and go to the Civic Center to receive their drive-through COVID test. Before leaving, Bria asked if I wanted to ride with them. I declined because I still needed to clean the house and start packing for our trip.

I called Haley at around 5 p.m. to see where they were and she responded, "At grandma and grandpa's house." She told me they would be heading home soon. I continued to dust and spot clean while listening to TV.

Around 6:00 p.m., all three of my children came home and sat in the family room. By this time, my husband was home and watching TV with me. During the next thirty minutes or so, each of my children were on their cell phones, looking at social media and texting. My niece and nephew were also at the house with us.

Bria (our middle child) offered to run by Portillo's to get me a strawberry shortcake. She was planning to drop it off at the house and then go over to her best friend's house for a couple of hours. She left, and the family room started to empty out as my husband went upstairs to watch a basketball game. Soon after that, Haley (our oldest child) eventually went upstairs to lay across the bed and talk to her dad.

Eric Jr. told me he was about to go work out and that he would return soon. I don't know what prompted me to do this, but I told him to come sit by me on the couch. I reached out my hand, and as he held my hand in his, he said "What?" I did not have a reason for wanting him to hold my hand. I do not know if it was a mother's intuition, or just a mother who wanted to hold the hand of her 18-year-old son who was her youngest and growing up so fast.

I gripped his hand, and he said jokingly, "A'ight now...I'll *be right back.*"

There may be nothing to it, but it is strange how we do not realize how little control we actually have over how our future unfolds. We assume that we have control and that we are coming back each time we leave home, but in reality, all we can do is hope.

I started to fall asleep in the recliner, but something woke me up at around 7:30 p.m. I grabbed the remote and started changing the channel to find something to watch when my phone made a sound. The sound was from private message sent via Facebook. I typically ignore Facebook messages, but on this night, I picked up my phone and clicked on it. It was from a person I did not know.

The message read, "Hi ma'am. Eric got in a bad car accident. They are taking him to OSF."

Pause.

"What?!"

I initially thought someone was pranking me, but then I thought, *Eric is not here!*

I jumped up, ran to the bottom of the stairs and yelled to my husband, "Eric! Someone just sent a message that Eric has been in a car accident!!" My mind had yet to catch up to what I had just said to my husband. He responded, "What?! Where?! Who sent the message?!" For some reason, at this point, I was starting to feel my body weaken.

I quickly read the message to him, told him that I did not know the person who sent it, and ran to my bedroom looking for my shoes. Well, my shoes were in a basket at the front door, but at this point, I was not aware of what I was doing. I was just trying to get my psyche to fall in line with what I needed to do – which was get to my child.

My daughter said, "I have his location!! He is on North Street! Let's go!" My husband and oldest daughter ran down the stairs and said, "Come on!" I kept pacing. I calmly said, "Go ahead. I'll be there. I'll be right behind you." They jumped into Haley's car in the driveway and sped away.

I think 2 or 3 minutes passed before I looked outside and saw my oldest sister's SUV in the front of the house. She was talking on the phone, but in front of my house because she was coming to pick up her children. I looked out the front door and just stood there. I think my mind was trying to process what was happening in that moment.

Something in my mind snapped back and I ran outside barefoot to her SUV screaming, "Something's going on with Eric!" The window came down as she held her cell phone. She asked me what I had said. She then hung up the phone and asked, "What happened?" as she jumped out. For some reason, I went back to a quiet space in my head and said calmly, "He was in a car accident, and someone sent me a message on Facebook saying they were taking him to OSF." I started to walk back in the house. She screamed for her children to get their shoes and coats on. She said, "Come on Bridgette, let's go!" I stood against the wall in the entryway and slid down it slowly and said, "I can't." I started to cry.

She grabbed my boots in the basket by the front door and said, "Put them on! We have to go!" I put them on slowly and told her my phone was ringing.

"Yes! Maybe it's my husband and daughter telling me that he is fine." I felt relief for a moment. When I picked up the phone, it was my aunt. She was crying and asking what happened to Eric. She was starting to see information on social media. I screamed, "I don't know! I got a message and we are going to the hospital. I don't know. I don't know. I don't know!"

When we got into my sister's SUV, my phone rang again. It was a cousin. My phone was dinging as messages were coming in from Facebook. My sister said, "He will be alright." I didn't say a word. I just sat there as she sped towards the interstate to get us to the hospital. Her daughter, then seven, asked, "TeeTee, is Eric going to die?" Trying to breathe at a normal pace, I said, "No."

My sister then told her kids to sit back because we needed to get the hospital as fast as possible to check on Eric. My phone was seemingly exploding as I answered call after call. I started crying again and I kept saying, "I don't know. I don't know what's going on. We're trying to get there."

We got onto the Interstate towards the hospital, and about 2 miles out, I noticed a lot of lights from fire trucks, police cars, and maybe an ambulance. I wasn't sure, and I looked up and said, "Oh, this night is crazy." What I did not realize was that those sirens were coming from the area where my son's accident happened. In my mind, I thought it was someone else. I started to think that maybe it was just a fender bender. I had no idea.

What was going to happen when I got to the hospital? I would not allow myself to believe that my son c could possibly die.

The night of the wreck, the Peoria Journal Star, wrote an article. Here is the picture included in the article.

Chapter 4

At the Hospital

As we pulled up to the hospital, the parking lot was full of cars. There were young people who were likely friends of my son and daughters, me and my husband's friends, and maybe some frenemies of my son in the parking lot huddled in different groups talking. I write that not to be mean spirited, but I am aware that everyone around during traumatic situations are not all there because of love. At that time and now, it doesn't matter to me why other people were really there. It only matters that I have gained a deeper understanding of the power of thoughts and the significance of understanding what's not significant. I needed the energy I had left to focus on whatever God was going to allow to happen next.

As we jumped out of the SUV, I saw that my husband and daughter, Haley, had already made it there. Bria received a call from her best friend (Haven), who told her that her brother had gotten into a car accident. She saw it on Facebook and called Bria immediately. Bria called Haley to find out what was going on and was headed to the hospital.

I thought, *Oh my God, I had forgotten to call my other child.* My mind was scattered. I could not think straight. I was a mess. We raced through the parking lot to the front. I jumped out of the car. My sister said she would park. I ran into the doors with my mask on. I saw my husband, and his eyes were red from crying.

I immediately asked, "Where's Eric?" He grabbed both of my arms and said very sternly,

"Bridgette, he's very, very hurt."

As tears rolled down my face, I asked, "What does that mean?" Then, I looked at the nurse and said, "I'm here to see Eric. He's my son. He's been in a car accident. Where is he?"

She said, "Let me call. He came in on a gurney in an ambulance."

I turned back to my husband, and I asked, "What is going on?"

There was a lady standing behind him and she had been crying. Eric said, "This is Eric's friend's mother. Her daughter was in the car with Eric."

"Oh my God, who, what?" I asked, "Do you know how my son is doing?"

She responded, very slowly, "Someone hit them while Eric's car was parked in front of my house with my daughter in the passenger seat. The driver of the SUV was driving very fast and when she hit the back of your son's car, the car flipped and hit a pole. Your son is very hurt. He was knocked unconscious as soon as they were hit."

As I listened to her, tears continued to fall down my face. I was having an out of body experience. I could not think. My body felt weak. I did not know what to say because I was in shock listening to her words and visualizing the incident in my mind.

Then a security guard came in, and he said, "Because of Covid protocols we can't let you stay in here. You have to go outside." I replied, "But I'm here to find out about my son." The nurse told the security guard to hold on, as she was waiting to hear back from the trauma unit.

The security guard repeated, "You have to stand outside, I'm sorry." So, we began to exit the emergency room area, and I saw my parents. My mother was running towards the emergency room doors as I started to walk outside. The security guard repeated, "I'm so sorry, you're just going to have to wait outside until the nurse gets an update from the trauma unit." At that moment, the nurse said, "Wait a minute, wait a minute. I have an update for his parents. I will never forget the intentional tenderness in her voice. She said, "They are still working on him."

I responded, "They're working on him? What does that mean?" I felt my body let go, then I fainted.

The security guard and my husband and mother helped place me in a wheelchair. As I began to come to, I said, "I can walk." The nurse then said, "One of you can wait in a waiting room outside of the trauma unit. My husband looked at me and stated, "I will go and wait."

The nurse then told us, "Here's the chaplain. He will escort his father to the waiting area."

I couldn't remember my own name at that point, if anyone had asked me. I couldn't remember my family, and I couldn't remember why I was at the hospital. My mind had gone completely blank.

The security guard brought a few chairs out for visitors to sit on as we waited outside. More people, family members, began racing into the parking lot, jumping out of their cars, hugging me, telling me it was going to be okay. I felt confused. I never had such a loss of thought before.

The day changed to night and my son went from being okay to fighting for his life.

Why was this happening?

At some point, one of my cousins walked up to me and asked me what was going on. I don't know if he had heard it from Facebook or not. At that moment, I could not speak. My mother and another cousin (Danita) just took over sharing updates as much as they could. They were also visibly upset but had enough strength to communicate on my behalf.

As I sat there, I quietly begged, "Jesus, please. Don't take my child. Don't take my son. He's the son I prayed for. God, please don't do this. God, please. Don't do this, God please. Don't do this. Take me. I will gratefully die, right here right now, if you would take me instead of him. I can't take it. Please, God. Hear my cry."

Then, I began to cry aloud with much more intensity. Everyone around me was quiet. They probably thought I was literally losing it. If they were thinking that they were right. I was losing my mental ability to understand the current state of the situation. This is one of the reasons I truly believe this book will be helpful to those who experience trauma. It may seem like you are losing it, but understand me and don't feel offended when I write, it is a choice. At first, shock set it for me, then I could not think at all, let alone logically. Though for me it was a slow process to gain enough of my mental consciousness to put the situation in perspective, the journey had to be traveled.

Realizing that I was on a new journey that I would not offer anyone to go with me on, I continued to pray. At some point, while I was praying, my other cousin (Pastor Steven McCall) called. I did not answer every call that came in at that point because I was praying, but when I saw his name, I answered. When I heard his voice, I felt like God was having him call to comfort me, because I was going to lose my son. I placed my phone on speaker so that everyone around could hear. As he prayed, I could tell he was crying as well. I kept crying then started to pray on my own again. My cousin prayed louder. He screamed out to God. He petitioned on our behalf.

During a point during his prayer for us, my mind shifted. I felt myself giving up and thinking, "God is going to take my child, and I don't know how I'm going to live." I laid my head back, and my eyes rolled back into my head. My mother was there, rubbing my back and talking to me as my father and my sister paced back and forth. My daughters were near, but did not know how to help me. Meanwhile, my other sister was making her way from Houston to Peoria.

In that moment, my mother must have felt my anguish. She must have felt that I was giving up. She separated me from the others and said, "Come sit in the car." I said, "I'm not cold." She repeated, "Come, sit in the car." I kept repeating that I was not cold and that I needed my child.

My mother used her strength, along with help from one of my cousins and a few friends, to lift me out of the chair and force me into the front seat of my sister's SUV.

I didn't put my feet inside; instead, I left my legs dangling out of the car door, while my mother wrapped blankets around me. I sat there crying, tears falling into my mask, crying out to God. I was still in disbelief, but at the same time, I was starting to accept that my son's death might be our reality. I had not heard from my husband yet, so I made my mind believe he was dealing with the loss and was going to walk out that front door and tell me that at I needed to walk in with him to see our son for the last time.

I sat up and looked to see my two daughters, holding each other. I saw my pastor and his wife pulling into the parking lot. One of my dearest friend and sorority sister was also pulling up. The lot was filling up with friends and family who were there to lend their support in prayer and encouragement.

It was in that moment that my husband called, and he said, "I'm going to text you before I call you with updates. Right now, what you need to know is that he's still alive. He's very hurt, but he still alive. Keep praying."

In prayer, I said *Thank you, Jesus! I'll take that. I came to realize that, clearly, making a deal with You is not going to work because I am still here, and You have not decided to take me yet, and my child is still alive.*

As the minutes and seconds passed, I again began to question Gods reason(s) for allowing any of this to occur. I asked, "So, what are you doing? Why are you doing this? He's a good kid. He's never been in real trouble. He is in your good graces. He's smart, he's handsome, he's witty. He's my child. I'm not perfect, but I've served. My family has served. Why would you break our family so tragically?" I literally went from begging God to questioning His intention. As you will read later in the book, the conscious mind impacts the unconscious mind in such a way that you choose a perspective based on many factors.

As I heard people who came into the doorway of the SUV, they continued to encourage me to stay strong while assuring me they were praying. I just glanced at all of the people around me - all of the family members and friends who are standing around shivering in the cold with their coats and boots on, some praying and some talking to one another. I still did not see what God was doing, but one thing I knew for sure was that there was love there. My village was present.

My husband called several times after each text to say our son was still okay and update me as the nurse kept updating him. He said the chaplain was there with him, but in my mind, I thought the chaplain's presence meant they were expecting my son to pass away, and my husband might need someone on hand to pray.

Chapter 5

Isolation Time

ecause of the first pandemic in my lifetime, COVID, I was not allowed to stay with my child in the ICU. A dear nurse allowed me to FaceTime him through Facebook. I saw a picture of my son with tubes, and I spoke to him as I cried. My husband and his sisters also talked to him. I saw his eyelashes move, and the nurse said, "He can hear you". I said, "I'm sure of it. Yes, I'm sure of it." The pain of not being able to be there to rub my child's head or hold his hand to pray over him was excruciating. It was an emotional pain that extended into my limbs, as my body ached as well.

My heart hurt. My emotions were beyond words. I wanted to vomit, but I could not. I wanted to scream, but I did not have the strength. It was hard to sleep. So, my husband, my daughters, a cousin, my sister, her children and I all slept in cars in the hospital parking lot. I wanted to be close as close to my son as I could. My parents would arrive every day and park next to us, and we would just put our windows down and talk to one another. I would call the hospital ICU floor, every three to four hours around the clock, to check on his status, find out the name of the nurse who was caring for my child, and to find out who took over as they changed shifts. Each time I spoke to a nurse, I introduced myself and let them know that I could not be there because he tested positive for COVID. I do not believe that my son actually had COVID. I do I believe that it wasn't meant for my husband, my sisters, or me to be physically present with my son. I did not know why then, but now, I have a clearer understanding of God's plan – not completely, but to some degree.

I prayed with my husband for our child, with our children, for their brother, with my parents, for their grandson, and with my sisters, for their nephew. These were the most authentic prayers I had ever prayed, and I came to know God in a brand-new way. It wasn't that He was brand new, it was that I became brand new.

I started to realize the things in life that no longer mattered. These were things that had mattered just a day or two prior to the accident. My mind wanted to hate the drunk driver who had hurt my son, but I couldn't. This was a miracle in the midst of COVID, and in the midst of our pain. God was showing us that He was present.

The struggle to see any situation in a positive way when others see it in a negative light can either show wisdom or naiveté. In the midst of trauma, most people view everything negatively. They wonder why the traumatic event is happening to them; some even believe the person or family is being punished for something. This is the cloudy thinking I mentioned earlier. When your mind is not clear and not centered on who and what matters most, you will be stuck in the valley. Nothing lives in that valley but confusion and despair. It is time to get out of the valley. It is time to get out of that quicksand and make your way to the mountaintop.

There were hours at a time that I isolated myself. I needed to be alone to think. I had to rationalize my thoughts. I needed to put the situation into context based on what I believed to be true about God. Even if you do not believe in Jesus Christ as I do, you need to believe in something higher and mightier than you. If you only believe circumstances exist or change because of you, life will prove to you how untrue that belief system is at some point in your life.

Isolation was not a time of loneliness for me. It was a time of reflection. I asked God to help me see the situation the way he saw it. I knew how much I loved my child, yet I truly believed and still believe God loves him even more. It is incomprehensible how much love was covering my child – especially when he was placed into a medically induced coma.

That time of reflection brought scriptures and situations back to my remembrance from *my* previous trauma. He reminded me that He was my Shepard and that He knew this event would happen exactly when and how he knew that it would. During the time I spent in isolation, I learned how to meditate.

In addition to breathing slower and with intention, I listened to the voice of God. He spoke to my thoughts, to my heart like I had never experienced. I came to understand that God was hurt because I was hurt, even though He knew the outcome. I began to feel peace as I felt the presence God near me. He held me so tight and reassured me that trusting His will was best for me. It eventually allowed me to sleep a little longer. I am sure the nurses were thankful for a little break.

For me, isolation gave me the strength I needed to calm my racing heart, decrease my anxiety, and receive emotional and physical rest by trusting in the promises of God. I knew that regardless of the outcome, God had already given me what I needed to make it. All of the situations I experienced over my life were just a prelude to what was the scariest event of my life. Every trial made me stronger. It sure did not feel that way during the trial, but I learned that the circumstances we endure make us a little wiser if we allow God to work through us. When we know through our belief system that a higher power is in control, we can release some of the emptiness we feel because we do not have to be what we truly cannot be in the first place – all powerful.

My son living or dying was completely up to God. I had to let go of my control and express my weakness so God could take over. When there is nothing else you can do, let go. If you know and believe in a higher power, let go sooner. It is not letting go of the person, it is letting go of fear and anxiety that will not improve the situation but will cause you emotional and physical harm in the end.

Chapter 6

Understanding Trauma

T his book is about living through, understanding, and dealing with trauma at its core. Trauma is a deeply distressing and disturbing experience that can occur with or without warning. It does not necessarily result in death, but it can. It does mean, however, that something so troubling has occurred in your life that you are trying to make sense of it. Sometimes it is living after a traumatic event and feeling the guilt of being alive when someone else you may know personally or may have heard of died, perhaps even from the very thing you endured. At some point in everyone's life, trauma will be experienced. How one deals with trauma determines whether or not one will be in a state of peace or distress.

Trauma affects people in different ways, at different depths, and at different times in their lives but one thing remains constant - trauma is often life changing. The change can be what you want it to be based on your place and the length of the time you spend in specific parts of the journey. We look at a journey of trauma using the following depiction:

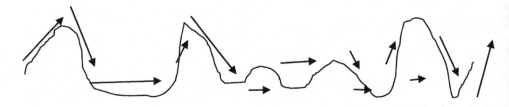

Somewhere between the hill and the mountaintop is where most of us reside when our lives are normal. We are not in distress; life is what most would call "fine" before our minds intrinsically understand that we are about to be emotionally hurt. Once we receive the news, we quickly descend to the valley, or the lowest part of our emotional state. At the beginning of most trauma, we stay in the valley longer than necessary. Most of us will remain in the valley until something changes. That change can be positive news or a better understanding of what is next, but regardless of what is next, we find ourselves typically back on the highest peak for a short while as our emotional state wanes with varying degrees of information.

Our journey is both emotional and physical. The emotional part, which is our mental state, is the origin of the journey. Our thoughts lead to the physical part of the journey. If we can understand the mindset, we can control the physical aspect of the trauma experienced. This is not to say we can fix physical ailments every time by thinking wellness, but there are many examples where mindset does connect directly to our physical bodies.

Sometimes we find that our emotions become stronger than our will, and we begin to experience anxiety and fear. If we live our lives mentally stuck in the trauma and what happened to us, worrying about how we are going to overcome, we will become captive to our negative emotions. There is not a magic process to deal with trauma as it is going on or during the aftermath of it, but there is a process that includes some valuable steps that I used as I went through my own trauma.

The Lesson I Learned: Understanding where you are on your journey is significant to understanding what your next steps to healing should be as you move forward. Draw your own journey. You may only be at the first hill, but you are feeling an emotional decrease as you deal with the pain. You thought you were getting better emotionally, then the negative thoughts came back. That's ok. Draw it out and stop where you are now. You will add to it as your journey continues. This is not a sprint in any sense; it is a marathon, and we must understand where we are on the journey to figure out how to prepare for the next part of it. What is your current mindset about the trauma you have experienced?

Chapter 7

The Impact of Trauma

*F*ear is connected to worry, and worry is connected to disbelief. Whatever has happened or is going to happen does not have a resolution - at least a resolution that we may find desirable. The Bible tells us to fear the Lord, and that i's the beginning of our knowledge. It took me years to understand exactly what that meant in the context of my life. I learned that it is not the fear we think of when we are afraid, but fear in reverencing and honoring something greater than you, something that has the power to end this world just as much as to create it.

In situations of trauma, there is often a significant amount of drama. Some of that drama comes from people who have direct details of the trauma, and some of the drama comes from those who do not. The problem is that the drama can sometimes muddy the waters and lead you and others who are called to action to be distracted from your assignment. Mental cloudiness prevents you from achieving your goal of getting to a place where prayer, connection, and repurposing the pain allow you to help yourself or anyone else.

Have you ever experienced trauma? Most of us have. They are varying degrees of trauma. The impact or the effect of the trauma on individuals depends on how the trauma is internalized. Some people can get to the other side of the trauma and repurpose it for a greater good, while others struggle.

Through our emotions, through our actions, and through our relationships, we learn how to cope with the issues in our lives that cause us pain. Some of us cope well and others fill the pain or the void with temporary satisfaction. Most who use negative coping strategies find that takes us back to place of despair, the place we were trying to desperately to escape.

The only constant in life is that everyone is on some type of journey, but most of us may not know where that journey is taking us. When somewhere along that journey, we experience heartbreaking experiences that lead to pain beyond what we believe we are able to handle, the trauma may make us question our belief systems. This requires us to analyze the pain from another lens.

I assert that learning to repurpose our trauma and find peace is the solution. The lessons that can be learned from it, and the changes that can occur in our lives, whether short or long term, can help us get to a place of understanding. Maybe not the *why*, but maybe to the point where we are healed and can help others heal. When we begin to see trauma through the lens of God, a God who does not create trauma to cause pain, but purpose, we find that there is some good that will come from it. As Romans 8:28 reminds us, good can come if the pain is connected to the will of God.

So how can trauma be a good thing? I am not stating that it feels good in the moment or even years later. Trauma can be used as a trigger to inform us of where we are on a journey - an individualized journey for those most impacted by the traumatic event(s).

How should we respond to that trauma? The truth is that the outcome of that trauma leads us in one of two directions – for the good or for the useless. If the end result of the trauma you are experiencing or have experienced does not encourage your emotional growth, wisdom, and empathy for others in similar situations, the trauma you experienced is useless. It's mostly useless because you are most likely still mentally trapped in negative thinking, which can lead to negative behaviors.

How was I able to find peace with the traumatic events that happened in my life?

Initially, I wondered why I was being punished. I knew there were people out there worse off than I – in terms of how they lived their lives, but why did it feel that *I* was being punished? In that emotional state, I was in the valley. I lived in that valley for quite a while. Fear, anxiety, depression, and disbelief reside with us in the valley. It causes us to think negatively and expect the worst. It is the part of our brain that causes thinking that is stuck in a place of sadness.

My thinking had to evolve.

I had to shift my perspective.

Chapter 8

Trauma to True Peace

*U*nderstanding how to get through trauma and get to the other side reminds me of the Biblical story of Peter being asked to walk on the water. As God stood in the middle of the sea, Peter was afraid to trust God because Peter thought he might drown, but while he kept his eyes on God, he could walk on the water. When he took his eyes off of God, he began to sink. And so was life. If we take our eyes off what gives us comfort, if we take our sights off that which can help us through the trauma, we sink. Some of us sink into depression, some of us sink into drinking or into drugs of abuse or other things that harm us physically and emotionally. That did not happen to me after my personal trauma, but after I experienced the trauma of almost losing my son.

My son lived, so why was I so depressed? Why was I self-medicating with sleeping agents to make me sleep? Why was I so untrusting of people? Why was I so paranoid that any of my three children could die at any moment? Why was I so afraid that God was going to make me prove my faith by taking one of my heart beats, my child? Why was I so afraid, when in this instance, he did not take my child and he had already shown me it was okay?

I wondered why I did not have the faith that I needed to have after God had already shown me how powerful he was and that this was only a portion of the story he wanted me to share with others. What was it about me that did not allow me to connect to an omnipotent, omnipresent, faithful, sustaining loving Father whom I worshipped? What was it that kept me from telling the story, everywhere I went? Wow, I thought. Is it because my son lived? Is it because I lived? Was it a story worth telling? It was, it is.

Chapter 9

The Guilt of Living – Survivor's Guilt

*J*t is the situation the living has to experience. How do you go from trauma that shakes you at your very core, that makes you so sick you cannot even vomit? The kind of pain of trauma that makes you cry six months later and your child is still breathing? What is it that gets you to the other side when you begin to sleep at night? What is it that gives you the peace that surpasses any understanding our finite minds can come up with? I will tell you what worked for me.

What is your pain? What have you gone through? What have you experienced that you cannot seem to reconcile in your mind? Once the pain gets into your mind, that means it has begun to work its way into your belief system. After you begin to believe it, you internalize it and begin speaking it. Finally, the pain is incorporated into your life, and you cannot see your way out of that valley. This is exactly what happened to me after my own illness.

When the pain takes over, your mind makes you believe that to numb it, you must do or take something to make the pain dissipate, if only for a while. I started taking pills - one before bed, then two before bed, then three before bed, then an additional one before going to work. I felt relaxed. I did not think it was a bad thing. In my mind, it kept me in a state of euphoria. I was wrong. I ended up depressed and dealing with survivor's guilt, as many people that I knew had passed away since the start of my own illness.

I could not understand how I lived. My first cousin, God sister, and best friend – all wrapped up in one - had died two years prior to my illness. She died from a freak accident caused by a surgeon who made a mistake that took her life. How did I get through survivor's guilt? I had to learn to trust the intentions of God. I had to reflect on His very character. I had to learn how to internalize the word of God in such a way that I could apply the lessons to my own life, realizing that my early assignment was not done. I had to seek the face of God in a way I had never tried before.

I screamed, I cried, I was shattered. I felt guilty. As I got through the anger and the guilt, I wanted to see the situation as God saw it. I prayed for that. And my prayer was granted. God knows the outcome of every situation. He knows the plan. We must stay on the journey and follow the path laid before us, trusting Him along the way so that we can find peace. If we remain in the valley too long, it becomes like the quicksand I mentioned earlier. You will sink so deeply that you cannot see your way out.

I made it through the valley of grief, to a land of peace, where I can not only talk about the situations that happened to me and my son, but also to where I can tell you about the survivor's guilt and PTSD, which are real things. They are real occurrences that can make you as depressed as someone who has lost a best friend to cancer, or who lost grandparents. It can make you as downtrodden as someone who has been backstabbed, used, and abused. I can tell you how I got over to that island of peace and hope where I am today, and where you plan to be. I will tell you how to get to a place where you can wake up and live out your day in total peace and worry less than those who do not have peace. I hope this is something you can experience.

To finally see the journey from the lens of hope, to finally sleep with dreams of fun stories and hope for the future, and to finally feel the fullness of this life God has for me and my family is nothing less than a miracle. I am not a miracle giver, but I believe God is. I believe that whether you are a Christian or not, whether you believe in Yahweh or something else, that you will get something out of this book. It will allow you to look at your journey, whatever it is, through a different lens, and know that however it turns out, it is okay. In the end, you will have peace.

Chapter 10

Beyond Fear

*T*here is not a magic process to deal with trauma as it is going on or during the aftermath of it, but there is a process that includes some valuable steps that I used as I went through my own trauma. As stated before, in the midst of those two major traumas, there were other significant events that happened. For example, family members died, some unexpectedly, some that most would consider too young with unfulfilled dreams. There is trauma that has occurred in my family in which the person did not die, but the situation was so painful that it was difficult to move past.

Dealing with a trauma can cause fear to set in. Once fear takes over your mind, other emotions, which are not connected to God begin to fill up mental space. Fear is connected to worry, and worry is connected to the belief that whatever has happened or is going to happen does not have a resolution.

The Bible tells us to fear the Lord and that is the beginning of knowledge, but it took me years to understand exactly what that meant. It turns out that fear is not the type we think of when we are afraid; the fear is in regard to honoring something greater than you, something that has the power to end this world just as much as it has the power to create it. When we learn to trust, then we can understand that we are not the ultimate determinants of our fate, and that is the beginning of understanding the importance of life.

When we look at fear and faith, based on the law of polarity are opposites in outcomes, but very similar in belief systems. When we are in a state of fear, we believe in something we cannot see, touch, taste, smell, or hear, yet it impacts the outcome of our situation because thoughts are powerful. When we are in a state of faith, we cannot see, touch, taste, smell, or hear and yet it also impacts outcomes. So, if we actually can shift our mindset to a belief system with something higher than ourselves (as I mentioned before), we can handle the outcome differently. It does not mean the outcome will be what we desire, it does mean, however, that we will have the capability to deal with the situation – regardless of the outcome.

We get to a point where we realize it is not just us and that everyone at some point will go through some level of trauma. The important part is that when we experience trauma, we have a source in which to seek that can provide comfort. We also have an assignment. This assignment, which I call a "Call to Action", is our responsibility for those with a heart to serve – help others who have been through something similar to your trauma. Tell them how you made it to the other side. If you do not seek to help others, this book is probably not for you because getting to peace involves moving beyond yourself and the circumstance. It requires pouring into others who are on the same journey or one like yours.

In trauma, there is often a lot of drama connected to the situation. Some of that drama comes from people who have direct details of the situation, and some comes from those who do not.

The importance of understanding the damaging effects of drama is that the drama can sometimes cloud the circumstances and lead you and others who are called to action to be clouded about your assignment. That cloudiness comes in the form of listening to people who don't believe in the higher power that you do; people who suggest negative outcomes before a real outcome is known. The list goes on, but the importance is understanding that these types of "interventions" prevent you from getting to a place where prayer, connection, focusing, and repurposing becomes a part of who you are as a result of the trauma.

A close friend of mine, whose child passed at the precious age of 19, once told me she is strong because it's not about what God does *for you*, but *it is about who He is*, and understanding there is something greater than you. There are forces greater than you, greater than the doctors, greater than the nurses, and greater than the circumstances. These forces somehow come together to make your life what it is, and when you begin to understand that, you are a little bit closer to understanding the mysteries that encompass our lives. You began to truly understand that even though there are people who think they are bigger than the universe, there are some things we cannot control, and I have shared two stories proving this fact.

What I realize, is that there are people in pain, whether it is emotional, physical, or psychological. Some people are reading this book who did not have a similar outcome. Maybe they lost their mother, their father, their child, or their friend. I have had some of those losses too, and maybe you are wondering, "How can I find peace? My child was in an accident and he or she actually died. They were a part of a tragic event, and they did not make it, so, how can you tell me how to get to peace?"

These two journeys that I have shared with you are not the only two journeys I have experienced. I lost a God sister who was as close as a real blood sister due to a simple surgery gone wrong. I lost a close friend to cancer. The list goes on. I have had losses and what I realized through all of the things I have been through is that there is still peace waiting for me. *Peace is also* waiting for you.

You just have to get to the other side of the trauma, and I am going to walk you through how I did that, after I went through two of the most difficult times of my life. These were not the only difficult times for me, but they were two of the most difficult times. I believe that life does not have to be complicated. God says, "Give me your burdens, give me your pain, cry on my shoulder, ask what you will in my name." We *choose* what we believe and which direction we go. I pray that you choose peace, love, and joy which resides in God.

The things we go through, which many times we cannot control, should make our relationship with God stronger. His burden is light, His yoke is easy. He just wants us to come unto Him.

Chapter 11

Understanding Peace

*W*hen I use the word peace, I'd like to use this as an operational definition. Peace for me includes the ability to accept and honor God's will, not just to react in my flesh. I needed to get to the other side of trying to figure out the *why*. I was asking about and experiencing the kind of mental state that resulted in learning thankfulness. In other words, peace is more than emotions. For Christian believers, peace results from acceptance to the will of God and obedience.

I and those involved were personally selected by God to see His glory and the end of that, for me, was freedom. My trauma contributed not only to my personal growth, but to the growth of many others. I do not believe that God created trauma to hurt us. I believe that there is a purpose *in and through* the trauma.

The Lesson I Learned: The experiences I have endured helped me to find the purpose of the bigger picture, and the lessons that needed to be learned through it. If you do not learn what you need to learn during one trauma, you may just have to experience another one. You must "see" the purpose in the pain.

The emotional revival that occurs in our mind as we gain insight through a change in perspective includes the notion that we trust in that which is bigger, more powerful, more loving, and more sustainable than our finite mind can grasp. Most of us get hope from that. I got hope from that. This is more about how I moved through that process with the help of God. As a result, I expanded my ministry to show others that circumstances may change, but you do not have to change negatively *with* them. And you may say, "but my child is dead, but my parent is dead, but I was in an accident, and I can't walk, something happened, and I can't talk, I can't hear, I can't see. So where do you find peace in that?"

The Lesson I Learned: You find peace in that which is higher than you and that which repudiates darkness in exchange for peace. The greater power, that is actually within you, can see the bigger picture. Understanding that life will happen whether you and I want it to or not will help you to understand we are here to serve a greater purpose.

My goal is to be transparent while showing God's plan for me and my family thus far. He is not a respecter of persons. He can do the same for you. My prayer for you and those who will hear about these stories, is that you will gain clarity and a better insight into God. And that because of your reverence for him, you will gain wisdom, and that wisdom will prayerfully lead you to peace.

Chapter 12

Getting to Peace....

Going from trauma to peace is a process that was difficult for me. It was a slow process, a process of understanding what I had been through and what my child had been through. It was getting myself to a place of solitude in the midst of all of the turmoil. To find peace while you are in it – whatever that "it" is for you - is something magnificent. It is something you will never forget once you get there because only those who get there know they are there.

Step one. I had to realize that there was something greater than my pain, something greater than me, and something greater than the doctors and the nurses. I had to trust that there was something greater than anything that lives in human form. I had to realize that there was something that was real, tangible, and omniscient. I had to realize that though I could not see him, I could feel him. I had to believe that the will of God was greater than my will, and although I had carried this child and pushed him out of my body, I did not create him. He was a gift to me, but he did not completely belong to me. My husband and I had to seek the will of God, recognizing that accepting His will, whatever it was, was okay.

I thought back to the story when God told the disciples that He was going to leave and that He was leaving peace. The Holy Spirit would be left as an in-between, to help us through good and bad times. We were to seek the Holy Spirit because it was going to be our comfort. I still wanted to know how peace that surpasses all understanding can exist. How can you have peace when you do not understand why things happen as they do? How can you have peace when your world is crumbling around you? How can you have peace when it hurts so badly? I knew who the giver of peace was. I just did not know how to get it, and when I finally got it, I did not know how to maintain it. How do I keep depression from creeping in? How do I not take these pills every night? Thinking that they were giving me peace. How do I stop the anxiety that plagued my every day, which seemed like every moment?

I realized that God is the nucleus that I needed to get to. He *is* love. But He is also peace. The beginning of me understanding true peace was my coming to the realization that He only wants what is best for us, and He is the only one who truly knows what is best. He would never do anything out of malicious intent, but only through love because He is love.

Once I realized this, I could act on it. I was raised in the church, and I praised a real God, but sometimes, real only seemed real on Sundays. Sometimes real is only when you are going through something, or you need something. What I did not realize until my own trauma began is that real is not just a genie in a bottle that does what I need it to do, when I need it to do it. I had to dig deep and realize that the God that I served was not a "him". It was not a feeling. It was not a pastor saying certain words that gave me chills. God is real.

He is as real as you and I. He is not a figment of our imagination. He is not something that we just read about in a book, whether it be in the Bible or somewhere else. He is as real as the wind moving across my face. He is as real as the leaves rustling. He is as real as the rain that comes from the sky in the evening. He is as real as my heartbeat in my body. He is real, and sometimes we must go through trauma to truly understand that.

As I remembered some scriptures that I have either read or heard in church, I began to truly understand that those scriptures had real meaning behind them. I remembered a scripture that said that He was a rock in a weary land, and one that said He healed the sick, raised the dead, died, and rose again. These words all became more than a Sunday school lesson to me. I finally understood that these things really happened, and that God can really do anything, because He is in control at all times.

God may not cause traumatic events, but He allows for them to happen. This begs the real question: Why? Why was he allowing this trauma in our lives? Why was he allowing so much pain? Not immediately, but in my reflection time, in my journal, in my observations, I began to understand that my pain, my trauma, my husband's pain and trauma, my children's pain and trauma, the pain and trauma of our family and friends, has a purpose. Wow. I did not know what that purpose was, but it was the first step for me. I had to accept that there was a purpose, and it was going to serve a greater good.

The Lesson I Learned: Know that the battle is truly not yours to win or lose. The battle belongs to God.

Chapter 13

The Intrinsic Need for Peace

*N*ow that God was understood in my heart to be more than just a figure talked about, preached about, and sang about, I knew that He was real and tangible. I was then able to understand the power of the greater good, and I had to reconcile the life of my son and the greater good if he lived. Could a greater good be served if he passed away? What about if he lived? The answer in both instances was yes, but what is that greater good? Is the greater good leading people to Christ, or perhaps helping people to become better people? Was it making us better people because of what we went through? I found during my journey that it was all of that. What I went through, and my family went through, all had to be repurposed in our minds. We had to retrain and reconfigure our minds to understand that went we went through was not futile. It was not to cause us heartache or keep us depressed. It was not to hurt us but rather to serve a purpose.

All of this does not mean that you will not experience pain. It does not mean that what you are going through will not hurt but repurposing the pain to understand that there is something greater happening in the situation means that you are on the right road to lead you toward peace.

The next thing I learned was how to repurpose the pain by speaking to the situation positively. In order for me to effectively do this, I had to use affirmations. I had to speak to the situation as though I was in control, although I knew that there was a power greater than myself involved that could make the situation go either way. In the Bible, we read the scripture that we need to allow us to meditate on certain things; whatever things are true, whatever things are noble, whatever things are pure, whatever things are lovely, and whatever things are of good report. If there is any virtue, if there is anything that is praiseworthy, meditate on these things. Meditate on the things which you learned, received, heard, and saw in God and in Paul, so that you can be filled with peace.

So, I meditated on those positive things. I stopped asking God to change the situation. I stopped asking God to tell me why this was happening, and I started speaking to those things which are true, those things which are God. If God as a healer decided that my son would live, then we would look back on this and it would be a testimony that God is a good, faithful, and just God. It would tell us that nothing can happen, life nor death, without God's approval. It would also tell us that God was merciful, and most importantly, that God loved my child, even more than I did. I had never said those things before, especially as it pertained to my life or the lives of any of my children. I love my children more than anyone or anything and I would die for them . I would give up my life without fault, without pause. In fact, it was God who did just that, because of his love for us, and I admit, as I spoke these positive things, I realized God loves my child more than I do, more than his father does.

God loved him most, and God would not allow anything harmful to come to him without being right there. I rested in that.

Did I still cry? Absolutely, between affirmations I did, because I was still trying to wrap my head around certain things, but to repurpose the pain is to put it in a positive light, to find light in the darkness. The darkness is negativity, but light is life.

The Lesson I Learned: By speaking the Word of God and believing it with my very being, I learned to look at the trauma through the lens of God. I began to speak the promises and truth of God. This allowed me to see my pain in that moment as that which can be a transformative moment for someone around me, someone reading what I wrote, someone watching me. When I began to see that others may be able to find God through the situation, I learned how to repurpose my pain.

The next thing I did was to rest in God. By breathing slowly, concentrating on my thoughts, and breathing my surroundings, I rested in God. When I forgot to control my anxiety, I turned to the scriptures. In Philippians, God told us to be anxious for nothing. Paul told us to be anxious for nothing, right?

The scriptures tell us not to put our faith in the flesh, but what things were game to me? Paul said in the Bible that he counted a loss for Christ. Yet indeed, I also count all things lost for the excellence of the knowledge of Christ. Jesus, my Lord, for whom I had suffered the loss of all things, count him as rubbish, that I may gain Christ and be found in him, not having my own righteousness. but that which is through faith in Christ. I need the righteousness, which is from God by faith, that I may know him in the power of his resurrection and the fellowship of His sufferings being conformed to His death. What this told me, in my stillness, and in my quietness, is that through the trauma and pain, God needed to get something from all of this. Whether He took my son or left him here, it was for me to understand the righteousness of Christ, and to have faith in that which is higher and more powerful than I. This is what God was seeking, in the midst of my pain. I then had to understand that if I was working toward this goal of having better understanding and trust in that which is higher than I, I needed to press on. So, whatever God had laid hold in front of me, I needed to press toward that.

I would think, "What is it that I'm supposed to get from this? Because my son right now is unconscious. So, what is it then? The family members, and those who love him, what are we supposed to gain from this?" We needed to all be of the same mind, which was to realize that God was in control and that He wanted us to see His righteousness and His glory through this situation. So, I rested in God and I asked Him for that peace. I asked Him to take the anxiety from me. I said to God, "I want to rejoice in you, but I'm hurting, Lord, what do I do?" In response, he sent a scripture that was known to me as a child to be anxious for nothing, but in everything in prayer and supplication with Thanksgiving let my requests be known to God and the peace of God, which surpasses all understanding, will guard my heart and my mind. My heart is where the gushy stuff is. That is where my feelings are. My mind is that logical thing that asks, "Why is this happening to my family?"

God said, "I protect them both, if you pray to me. In supplication, give me all of you. Cry out to me. Don't look for your pastor. Don't look for your parents. Don't look for your spouse. Look for me, and I will give you everything you need, even peace. I'll allow you to laugh at a joke that someone's trying to make to change the atmosphere, but what's really happening is that you're learning more about me. You're learning to trust me. You're learning to see my righteousness, even as the tears flow down your face."

The Lesson I Learned: If you did not plant it, nothing can grow. If you did not or do not plant the Word, you live in a land of desolation. God cannot multiply what does not exist. You can only rest in that which exists to you. It cannot exist in you if you do not have a connection with that which is higher than you.

Chapter 14

Let Go by Internalizing and Living from the Word of God

s the time passed, and the calls continued to come every 30 to 45 minutes from my husband giving me updates on our child, I was slowly starting to release positive energy by talking to family and friends around me. I closed my eyes, and I said, "Lord. Let your will be done on Earth, and please Lord, give me the strength to endure whatever is next." Within an hour of that silent prayer, my husband sent a text saying our son was alive, and he was about to call. When my husband called, I placed the call on speaker, and he stated, "They are taking him to the ICU. He is critical, but he's gonna live!" I placed both hands in the air and quietly said, "Hallelujah. Hallelujah. Hallelujah. Praise You, Lord. We thank you for your goodness and your mercy that surrounds us. We praise you for who you are!"

Affirm the Word through prayer, through speaking, and in your thoughts. We hide the Word in our hearts, so we do not sin against God. If I never let it go, I have held on to something God wants me to release as my trust and faith in Him grows. Trust Him in the midst of the trauma. Even while crying, yell out the Word of God to God. Scream out His promises. Tell Him you trust Him and believe He is doing what is best in that very moment. Speak to God in real time, with real emotion, and real intention.

Healing is getting to the place, where you truly understand in your soul that the outcome of the situation does not mean God has left you. It does not mean that you or someone else is being punished. It is understanding that when you trust God to supply all of your needs, which includes living your life without a loved one and still leaning and trusting God, you are beginning to understand *who* He is. At this point, you can find peace, whichever way it goes. This is when you are beginning to get heavenly wisdom. It means you realize that when you cannot control the situation, you might want to get out of the way and let God handle it. It is when we are at our weakest that God can do His work on us.

It is when we are at our weakest, that we can be the most transparent, the most authentic- our real selves. When we are weak it does not matter who is around or what people are saying. All that matters is that we hear the voice of God and that we believe that voice, and believe that however it turns out, He was in control the entire time. Knowing that He loves us more than we love ourselves leads us to the road called peace. It helps us to get control of our emotions knowing that God is protecting our hearts. It helps us to stop the anger knowing that God is going to do what He is going to do because he is guarding our mind. It helps us to focus on the positive things about the situation. The negativity is darkness, and we want to be in the light.

It has now been over a year since that fateful night. It started off dark, and then the sun began to rise, and my hope in the Lord grew, not because my child lived, but because God lives.

Chapter 15

The Paradigms
That Impact How We Heal

To understand paradigms in the context in which I am using it is to first understand the power of our mind. The mind is very powerful. God is the greatest Creator, but the mind is one of the greatest creations. As we evaluate the conscious and subconscious mind, let us analyze them from two separate constructs that together impact how we endure trauma, find peace, and keep or discard our everyday habits.

We will start with the subconscious mind. It is that part of our mind that accepts what our conscious mind tells it based on factors I will address in this chapter. The subconscious mind is programmed in essence with what many coaches call a paradigm. We can therefore use an operational definition of a paradigm by considering the subconscious mind a multitude of habits. Habits, we can conclude are those thoughts fixed in our subconscious minds that surfaces as situations occur in our lives. We typically act on those habits, stored in our subconscious mind without a lot of deliberation, because they are essentially planted there from our conscious mind.

As I think about my son and his friend being hit by a drunk driver and hearing that he was unconscious and they were working on him, my subconscious thoughts were that he might not live. My reactions to hearing bad news about his condition at that time were those of despair and hopelessness. How did this paradigm develop?

Most would argue from past experiences, news stories, and other events in which something similar or tragic happened to someone else, and the result was death. Our brains can sometimes be programmed from our environment when we are children.

After we get older, our conscious minds our built. The conscious mind has sensors (hear, smell, touch, and taste. The difference with our conscious mind is that we now have what we call intellectual factors which allow us to make decisions. We now have intuition, perception, imagination, and all of the tools we use to make informed or ill-informed decisions. The things that we think are generally those connected to the paradigm, which is made up in our subconscious mind.

I would suggest that how I initially reacted to hearing of the wreck was one of panic. This was partly because I did not have all of the information. When we do not have all of the information, which we rarely do at the beginning of a traumatic event, we pull from the subconscious paradigm that was developed as a younger person. The paradigm then controls our body vibrations and causes us to feel and react in a way that is in alignment with what we currently have planted in our subconscious mind.

As one of my coaches explained, the law of vibration states that everything moves; nothing rests. Our bodies (including our minds) are constantly vibrating. The energy that flows through our minds causes this vibration, which connects with our senses, and ultimately causes us to make choices on how to react to a specific situation. We can choose a negative reaction or a positive reaction.

This is why you can find people who are not willing to forgive others, have low self-esteem, decide to murder someone without thinking about consequences stay in the same space for many years. This is also why you can find people with college degrees lack basic intelligence when it comes to things like helping others, making wise decisions about their lives, and so on. Can we change that paradigm in our subconscious mind even though it has been there for a long time? The answer is yes. You have to first understand and believe that your reactions are directly connected to your mind – both your subconscious and your conscious mind.

Chapter 16

Changing Our Paradigms

*W*hen I thought about the possibility that my child might die, I thought about it through my conscious mind. From there, it flowed to my subconscious mind and changed the vibration of my entire body. This all led to my feeling an out of body experience. Another example is that when someone says something unkind to us, we *choose* how we will react. It is controllable when we understand two things – how the brain functions and the connection to faith, which I will discuss soon.

We have to be committed to changing the results that come out of us, which means addressing our minds and how they can be changed for the better. Even though thoughts originate in our subconscious mind and it sends the vibrations and energy through the body, resulting in our actions, it is the conscious mind that tells our subconscious mind what to do and how to respond. Our subconscious mind cannot truly differentiate between what is real and what is unreal because it has been programmed over the years. The only way to change the subconscious mind is to change the paradigm that lives in the subconscious mind. Once this has been accomplished, the conscious mind can see, hear, and smell but when that information is translated into the subconscious mind, the subconscious mind makes the decision to react based on how it has been reprogrammed.

As life happens in real time, our conscious minds develop thoughts based upon something that has occurred and it has two choices: To choose that which is negative or that which is positive. We will call the negative side the one where insufficient information has been gathered. The positive side is where the conscious mind has informed information. This is beyond intellect. This is about changing thoughts and replanting the right information and allowing it to grow in our subconscious programming so our behavior can change.

This has allowed me to experience peace by kicking fear from my mind. I intuitively knew that God was omnipotent, but my subconscious mind included doubt, which grew into a triplicating fear. I learned that prayer to God was where the power lived. It was my faith in God and desire to learn more of Him and believe every promise He made that allows me to this day to know my paradigm has shifted. It is not the outcome of the situation that should control our complete mind, it is the will of God that should overtake our senses and cause us to respond with the understanding that God is omnipotent. His omnipotence allows me to rest my mind as I isolate in fervent prayer to that which is my higher power.

The Lesson I Learned: We must first have the desire to change, then we must be connected to faith in a higher power. This is about 90% mindset and 10% strategy. Desire to change your mindset, then work on your mind – all while building your belief and faith in a higher power.

Chapter 17

The Testimony

God does not leave us…He is right there. It is a matter of whether we take him with us on our journey.

Life's journey is long and often complicated. I have asked Him where He was when I needed him most.

He responded, "I was there all of the time."

God is not impressed with people who think they are more than they are.

Our purpose is not to boast about ourselves, but to worship and praise God while telling the world of His goodness – not because of *what* He does, but because of *who* He is.

If what we do does not glorify God, it is all in vain.

Whether people speak it or not, we are vessels, here to serve His purpose….

My illness was not so that people could come around cry and wonder why God would let this happen.

It was at that point, during the critical moments when my son and I were on death's doorstep, that God wanted everyone to see Him work miracles.

We often miss the lessons that we are supposed to learn in life–only to repeat the mistakes from yesterday.

Whether it be sickness, sadness, or something else, we ought to ask ourselves, "What am I supposed to learn from all of this?"

Nothing *just* happens.

God is in control of all things.

Coincidence is make-believe. God is real.

We are living testimonies!

But do we keep it to ourselves, or do our life and words reflect that we recognize every thought, movement, or action is by the grace of God?

He does not need us, we need Him.

He is God, all by Himself.

Once we realize that we are vessels by which God's word is spread, we begin to decrease as God increases.

His increase allows us to turn our concentration away from what has happened to us physically and focus on what He is doing spiritually and what He wants us to gain from it.

If the situation is profound enough to cause us pain, whether it be through tears, or any other sort of heartache, God is really trying to speak to us.

When someone goes through sickness, it is not just that person that God wants to reach, but everyone who witnesses it and becomes a part of the process....

To know that *He is all* is overwhelming for some and unpracticed belief for others.

God has power that no one else possesses. His love for us cannot be measured…he loves us more than we could ever love ourselves.

God is everything we need! He is all! He has been my father, my mother, my sister, my brother, my best friend, my boss, my teacher.

When I get lonely, He comforts me.

He does everything for me every day that most would not do for me once a year.

He will listen when no one else will.

We have to ask ourselves, have we experienced God, or do we live in the trauma we are experiencing?

There is a such thing called Justice, but there is also a thing called Mercy…

To experience God is to learn about Him, and when you learn about who He really is, you have no choice but to love Him.

God's grace is sufficient. We must see His strength when we are at our weakest moments.

We know that God causes all things to work together for the good of those who love God and are called unto His purpose (Romans 8:28).

To God be the Glory…forever and ever… Amen.

While my illness was a life-changing moment for me, God was not yet done with the experiences that would change the very fabric of our family.

God had another puzzle piece to make my journey a complete story. Not only did I experience trauma directly as a patient, but God decided He was going to show me the other side of the trauma. So now, I have the perspective as both a patient and as a spectator for another person's trauma. This book is not just about me discussing my personal trauma to you. It is also me talking to you through these words to let you know that we all go through various levels of trauma. How we deal with it in the midst of it all, as well as afterward, determines who we become, what our life becomes, and what meaningful experiences happen next in our lives.

Chapter 18

Time to Confront the Drunk Driver in Court

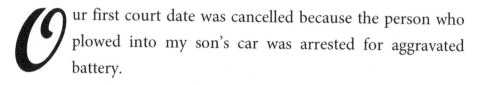ur first court date was cancelled because the person who plowed into my son's car was arrested for aggravated battery.

The case then moved from traffic court to felony court.

The defendant was initially charged with four felonies: two felonies for each person in the vehicle.

A few months passed, and we received notice that three of the felonies were dropped in the plea deal made between the State's Attorney's Office and the Public Defender's Office. The defendant was looking at a maximum of five years, instead of 15-20!

We finally received a court date, and 12 or so family members could attend the midday sentencing hearing.

I cannot really say if I was mad, scared, or indifferent. I can say that I was emotionally and physically drained, but I was also curious.

I had only seen the defendant in a picture in the Commitment Report for the police department.

As I sat there, I watched a young, short, child-like woman walk into the courtroom. She had on an orange jumpsuit. She came in with shackles around her ankles. I watched her every move. She walked slowly as though she was walking into a situation she did not want to be in. She walked unsure, as if she was unclear of the purpose. She walked looking down the entire time – never looking up to see who was in the courtroom.

I was allowed to read my impact statement to the court from the witness stand.

This is the letter:

To The Honorable Judge Kevin Lyons,

*Re: **Case No: 21-CF-XXXXXXX***

I am the mother of Eric L. Heard, Dr. Bridgette Heard. My son and his friend were sitting in my son's car around 7 p.m. on December 18, 2020, watching a video on my son's phone before pulling off to go to the gym. During that time, a Tahoe SUV speeding down North Street without headlights barreled into my son and his friend, causing the Camry to flip over before sliding and plowing into a light pole.

I received notice of the accident via Facebook Messenger from a friend of my son's around 7:20 p.m. Upon hearing of the news, my husband and one of my daughters ran out of the house. My daughter had his location on her phone, so they were enroute to North Street. I, still at the house for a few moments longer, slid down the wall in my hallway in disbelief. I was incoherent. I was in shock even though at that time I did not know how bad it was.

My sister and her two children put on my boots and got me into her vehicle as we sped to OSF. My phone was ringing constantly as pictures of my son's car were added to Facebook and people began writing about the horrific scene. My mind was so foggy, I even forgot to call my other daughter, who was on the way to a restaurant. She found out from her best friend, who saw the information on Facebook.

Upon entering the hospital ER, my husband and his friend's (name redacted) [name redacted] mother were at the nurse's station, trying to get more information on the condition of the kids. I was told by [name redacted] mother, who was also crying, that my son was knocked out on impact and she did not know if he was ok, but, "It was bad," she stated.

Crying, I asked the nurse to please tell me if my son was ok. I gave her his name. At the same time, a security officer told us that we could not remain inside because of COVID restrictions. As we began to comply, the nurse met us as we were walking out and stated that he was in the trauma unit, and they were "working on him." I remember repeating her statement, but in the form of a question, I asked, "Working on him? What do you mean?" – then I fainted.

The hospital sent the chaplain down to talk to us. At that time, they would only allow ONE parent in the trauma floor waiting room to get updates from the doctor. My husband and the chaplain went to the waiting room together. As I came to, I was placed in a wheelchair and sat outside in the cold with around 40 other people – both friends and family, waiting to see if my son was going to live. I could not even sit in the waiting room with my husband of over 25 years to get updates.

My husband had to provide updates to me...His first text to me stated, "He's alive...I am about to call...then he would call." The first call was that they were trying to stabilize him, but he was in critical condition. The second call was that his lung collapsed. The third call was that he had *fractured ribs and a broken collar bone. The fourth call was that he had a bad concussion. The fifth call was that he had to be given more blood. The six call was that they had to put a breathing tube down his throat to stabilize his breathing. The seventh call was that they were transferring him to the ICU, and he was still not responsive. They put my 18-year-old child in a medically induced coma, and because of COVID, I could not visit him for 7 days. We waited 3.5 hours to find out he was even alive! The anguish that I felt, my husband felt, his two sisters felt, his grandparents, aunts, other family members felt, was unbearable. It was an out of body experience for me.*

For 7 days, I called the hospital every 3-4 hours, every day. I talked to every nurse that treated my son. I even asked to sign a waiver that if I contracted COVID, there would be no liability on the hospital. They would not let me touch my son, so I slept in my car in the hospital parking lot – to be close to my child.

On day 3, they began to wake him, and we were allowed to see him via Facetime. I included a picture with this statement. To see my son with a tube in his mouth, unresponsive, took my mind to a place, it has yet to recover from.

On Christmas morning we were able to pick our son up from the hospital. He did not know what happened to him. He had a look of shock on his face like he did not know who we were. My heart still aches from that moment.

A nurse, by the name of Caronda (last name omitted), reached out to me while my son was in the hospital to find out if he was alive. She was so afraid he had not survived the wreck. She and her husband saw the Tahoe driving down North Street at a high rate of speed (with the headlights off). As their light turned green, they turned and saw the entire accident happen. She asked her husband to pull over. She jumped out of the car to assist. Neighbors were apparently yelling at her not to touch my son. She told them that she was a nurse. As she got into the car as much as she could, she grabbed his wrist. He had a faint pulse. She pushed herself into the car more and adjusted his head – raising his chin so he could breathe. I know that if she had not seen the accident and tended to my son, he would be dead.

Maybe you think I should just be grateful that my son is alive. I am forever grateful that Jesus Christ used the doctors and nurses to save the life of my child.

The only problem is…I have a different child.

My child is suffering from depression, sleeplessness – likely due to his brain injury. He can't play basketball, because to repair his collarbone they had to re-break it and insert a metal plate with rods. The metal plate and rods will be in his body for the rest of his life. The plate sticks out and people can immediately see that he had a major injury.

I pray that defendant pays for her crime. On paper, she did not kill anyone. In life, she killed me and my family. We will never be the same. Beyond the extreme anxiety for which I am taking medication, my son is not the same. That major concussion has led to mood swings, depression, and the inability to sleep.

The defendant does need help. If she does not pay for her crime, the next time she comes before a judge, it will be for another DUI that results in murder of someone else's family member. This woman not only hit the car of my son with him and his friend inside; she got out of the SUV and ran!

She left them for dead. She had the wherewithal to know to run...unbelievable.

I ask the court to give her the maximum sentence allowed by her plea deal. She needs and deserves to serve 5 years...at a minimum.

A lesson not learned will be repeated.

Thank you for your time,

Dr. Bridgette Heard, Wife of Eric Heard - Mother of Eric, Haley and Bria Heard

The defendant received the maximum allowed by her plea deal – five years. She has been remanded to the county jailhouse where she will serve 85% of the five years, with 121 days of time served. Do I have peace with her sentence? Yes.

My peace is not connected to the circumstance. My peace is connected to the creator and giver of life that helped renew my mind.

The Lesson I Learned: I planted seeds of faith in the ground that are now growing. As life happens, I have the armor to fight the goal of the enemy to enter my mind, corrupt my thinking, and make me believe that God cannot do something with what is happening in my life during a traumatic event. Peace can only come from that who created it and can provide it and for me and my family that is Jesus Christ.

I pray that the young lady finds a better way to deal with her issues. I may not understand *why* a lot of things happen, but I do understand *who* allows things to happen. Knowing the *who* provides a mind-settling acceptance and belief that things have turned out just as they are supposed to, and that gives me a peace that I cannot explain beyond that.

Chapter 19

The Trials That Make Us Stronger

*J*n the Book of James, we are told to count it all joy when we go through trials because the testing of our faith produces patience. For some of us, we have to go through trials for us to call on God with a sincere heart. Some may ask how can we trust God when we can't trace him? It's faith. Remember, we choose between fear and faith. They both are the same in that we don't have the five senses to make them what the world sees as tangible, but I declare that the outcomes for your life are different, based on your choice. Should you choose faith in the Divine, you will begin on that part of the journey that leads to spiritual maturity. From that spiritual maturity, you will gain an understanding. That understanding means a change in your mindset.

The change will allow you to react to trauma differently as you experience it. It is unlikely only one trauma will be an experienced by a person, but it is absolutely likely that if we have the spiritual and mental tools to assist us in seeing the trauma/incident from the lens of God. As a result, we get stronger every time we need to disregard man's logic and focus on God's logic – which is that everything happens in a specific season for a specific reason. It does not mean I completely understand why we were chosen, but it helps me to understand that because God allowed it to happen, He knew why. I understand that He knows all and controls all, and because of that, my Father has complete control – especially when it looked like He did not. He really did have control I have learned to have confidence in God through my prayers, talking and listening to him, and knowing He is everything that He tells us He is and can do whatever He says He can do. The issue for many of us is, what if He decided not to do what we desire? We know that our Divine Father is able, but if he chooses to do what He has the right to do, which is take our loved one back to his or her heavenly home, we have to accept his will. We know His will is perfect, even when it appears imperfect to us.

The Lesson I Learned: Faith precedes Sight. We must have a connection to God then we can develop the faith to make it through the situations that cause us to fall to our knees crying out to God that we will accept His will and to help us either way it goes. I had to do this. It was the hardest thing I did that night. I knew they were working on my son to keep Him alive, but I also knew (when I was able to come to myself mentally) that it was really all in God's hands. It did not matter how hard they tried. The decision of whether my son stayed on this early a little longer or went back to his heavenly home on December 18, 2020, it was because God had the final say. I had to be ok with that. As a mother, I cannot fully explain how painful that was to give it over to God. To completely give it to God and wait in faith for God's answer.

We have to let go of past and current hurts. It is letting go of your misconception that you can do it on your own. If you do it on your own and it works, believe me, it is by chance. Trusting God is not a roll of the dice. It is as sure as you reading this book. It is as sure as me writing it right now when I should be six feet underground in a cemetery without the prayers of those who know and believe in a living God. And most importantly, in God granting their request. It is the very same thing for my son. His life is not his own. It is not mine. We belong to God. When it is our time, we will go, but until God says so, we will serve Him and help others to know that you must have a connection to the Divine as you are incapable of mentally addressing those things that cause negative thoughts and actions without His help.

It is so important to teach our children that trusting God will help us through moments when we cannot think of one single person to turn to. It will be our lifesaver when we feel as though we are drowning from this world's attacks.

I *learned* and *lived* the Word that has allowed me to speak with confidence that God can't fail. Even in our worst circumstances, God *can* bring us out!

Most of all, I thank God, my way maker, for sending us! We have grown spiritually because we have focused on meditation, prayer and as a result have learned how to change our mindsets as it relates to what we will accept and what we will not accept to believe.

One of my favorite scriptures I like to read aloud before I begin to meditate is below. If you are a believer, find a scripture that speaks to your heart. It may be a scripture that relates to your current situation or it may be a scripture you just ran across and loved. Make sure the scripture has meaning for you, read it slowly, think about what it says to your spirit, breathe, relax, read it again and pray. When you pray, take time to listen to God. If you sit silently and focus, you will hear from God.

Bless the Lord, O my soul; And all that is within me, bless His holy name! Bless the Lord, O my soul, and forget not all His benefits; who forgives all of your iniquities, who heals all your diseases, who redeems your life from destruction, who crowns you with lovingkindness and tender mercies, who satisfies your mouth with good things so that your youth is renewed like the eagle's [Psalm 103; 1-5].

I pray this book has been a blessing to you and provides you the right tools that will allow you and your tribe to take the journey, realizing there are many parts of it. Some parts you will walk alone, and during other parts of the journey, there will be people who are of help to you.

The bigger picture for you is to shift your perspective and repurpose the pain.

Chapter 20

Next Steps...

*J*t is my heart's desire is that this book has provided introspection into my life as a mother that has s overcome traumatic events – with my son's car accident as the most devastating to me. You have read the stories, possibly felt the pain, maybe understood the journey, but are still left with the question of how you get through to the other side.

I hope that I did not make it seem easy, because it was not. I struggled writing this book for a while because it took me back mentally to a place where I thought I had recovered.

I realized that the timing was wrong. I could not write a book about healing, until I was healed. So now, after eighteen years of going through my own trauma and a little over a year of dealing with the trauma from the events that hurt my child, I can write about it with confidence. I can write about it with the assurance that those who know hurt in an incredible way can find rest in the arms of Jesus, regardless of how the situation turned out.

For the sake of making this book comprehensible for all, I want to briefly address the importance of understanding and leaning on a source greater than you – as I stated before, for me and my house that source is Jesus Christ. I would also like for you to work on your mindset. For some, this will mean intense, professional therapy. I believe in God wholeheartedly and believe if you find the right psychiatrist for you, that is a great pairing. None of it will work, however, until you have a mental paradigm shift.

Understanding the power of thought is an important part of healing. The Bible tells us so as a man thinketh, so is he. Our thoughts can help or hinder us. Remember, our initial thoughts live in our subconscious mind. As a baby, our subconscious mind is formed first. This is where our habits develop based on various situations and environments. The great news is that we can change our subconscious mind to believe what we want we need it to believe if we are able to change our habits.

Our minds will first reject changing certain habits, because our brains are used to doing certain things a specific way – and there have been a lot of years of habitual practice. So how do we change our habits? We change them through desire and persistence. We have to have a real desire to change them. Where does that desire come from? Persistence – in other words, repetition. Repetition is a trainer that allows our minds to question our previous thoughts and develop new subconscious thoughts that become actionable, conscious thoughts.

Your desire to change your thinking must be so strong, that it could be classified as an obsession. Once you are obsessed with the promises of God, positive thoughts, good deeds and so forth, your mind is starting to get the message.

Have you ever asked yourself why people react differently to bad news, trauma, and other life issues? It is primarily because their minds have been programmed by what has been entered into it. Your mental paradigm is situated so deeply in your subconscious that it has a stronghold on your habits and behavior. Those multitudes of habits emerge in your character. They emerge when you are happy or sad. They emerge when you are shocked. Our mental paradigms even have an effect on how we see ourselves and others.

If you want to work on changing your life, I encourage you to follow the steps that I followed on my journey. You may also want to document your progress in a journal as I did. It was an amazing experience read from one day to the next of how I began to realize I was on a spiritual journey. Jesus was right there as He was changing me while I was on a path that I thought was going nowhere.

I would submit to everyone reading this that these steps work for many situations, not just when going from trauma to peace, but if you want to go from one place in your journey to another. Getting to the place we want to be is a matter of getting from the mental state we are in to the mental state we want to be in. To do that, we must address the intermediary problems that are preventing us from getting from one point to the next.

We have to understand that we become what we imagine. If we expect a bad outcome, it is likely that we will receive a bad outcome. To the contrary, if we expect great outcome, we may get a great outcome, but even if we do not, we have planted seeds of positivity in our minds that will allow us to handle the outcome from a positive perspective, even it is not what we desired.

Another important point is that our minds become obsessed about the situation which we think about repeatedly. in an obsession That obsession can turn into desire, which triggers emotion and lead to action. This is a worthy road to travel if we are obsessed over that which is positive.

Immediately following my son's accident, subconscious mind crowded with negative thoughts connected to sickness and trauma, it is not healthy. It is not healthy for you mentally nor physically.

All of the listed above my thoughts were at that time were connected to a negative outcome. My subconscious mind told my conscious mind that this was the likely outcome, so I reacted as though it were true. I cried, I fainted, I fell to the ground, I kept asking God to save my child – my only son. I stated that phrase over and over again. Are you seeing the repetition?

Deep in my subconscious were those scriptures I had learned as child in Sunday School, listening to the pastor, listening to church music and so forth. I started rejecting the negative emotional statements and feelings with the positive ones, and as my mother rubbed my back and my cousin prayed aloud, my paradigm began to shift. I started crying out to God. The Word of God began to get louder than the whispers of the enemy.

I had a desire for my child to live. I became obsessed with him living. I started to speak back to God what I had read, I knew that the people (including me) who were called by His (Jesus) name- yep, me, would humble themselves, pray, seek His face, turn from their wicked ways, so they (I) would hear from Heaven – and that same God would heal their (our) land.

There were so many scriptures that began to come to the forefront of my consciousness because I kept repeating them over and over and believed every word.

At the point where I stopped, I prayed that God's will be done. The only thing I asked of Him is that He would give me the strength to make it through whatever He decided to do. *That is when the breakthrough came.*

Please understand, it is more than saying words, it is believing them. It is changing your mental programming to divert from what you are used to saying and believing to what you know to be true, regardless of the outlook. The most difficult thing I have ever had to do as a mother was say to God, I would accept His will, if He took my son. I meant it. It brings tears to my eyes as I type, but I had to look at the truth of the matter – our children do not belong to us. They are gifts from the Lord. My child was given to us, and the Lord had the right to take him back home. We must stop trying to bargain our way to blessings. We have shift our thinking to realize that we are not in control.

If we are going to change the paradigm,

- We must know our thought patterns.

- We must create new, positive, actionable thought patterns.

- We have to make a committed decision that nearly everything we have been taught, may have been wrong.

- We have to create, develop, and sustain the paradigm shift by constantly repeating the new things that bring positivity into our lives.

- We must make those subconscious thoughts conscious thoughts, by bringing those thoughts to the forefront of our minds. This occurs through belief and repetition.

As my mindset shifted, here is how my thoughts were conveyed from the subconscious to the conscious mind:

Shock ⟹ Calmer (It was not instantaneous, but it did come.)

Fear ⟹ Trust (I trusted God and the process He was allowing us to go through.)

Worry ⟹ Contentment (My trust in God took away the worry.)

Anxiety ⟹ Hope (My hope was in God and a positive outcome.)

Loneliness ⟹ Companionship (I had family and friends, but God was the companion that comforted me.)

Heartbroken ⟹ Mended Heart

Hopeless ⟹ Hopeful

Anguish ⟹ Delighted

Sadness ⟹ Joyful

Sorrow ⟹ Happiness

Nauseous ⟹ Healthy

Angry ⟹ Peaceful

Suicidal ⟹ Full of Life

I am not suggesting you would describe your journey in any of these words. This was my journey and how I felt from the time I found out about the crash until very recently. I do suggest, however, that you write down how you felt initially and how you are going to replace those emotions with positive words that will translate into powerful, positive actions.

I am also not suggesting that I went from one mindset to the next on the night of the crash, when my son was released from the hospital, or even a year later. Some of the shifts in my mindset have occurred recently. It takes time. You will know when you are ready to share your story when you have a full mindset shift and your paradigm is helpful to you, regardless of the circumstances.

I pray that your life will dramatically accept the new things that have been placed in your spirit that will bring you joy, fulfillment, and ultimate peace as you travel the journey God has planned for you.

A prayer:

I pray for the one reading this right now....

Father, someone reading this might be going through a storm. They are on a part of the journey where they don't know if should turn back or if they can or should keep going. They do not know why there is so much pain. We have read that you know all things and can do all things, Lord we have read, that you are All...We come to you as humbly as we know, thanking You for being God...We thank You because without You, there is no other help we know. We ask that you help us develop a mindset that reflects your love and your ways. We reject the negative thoughts that come to cloud our minds and distract us from listening with all of our hearts to you. Help us to accept your will in our lives and to be of service to others in need of restoration.

We understand that You never promised this road would be easy, and because we know You are in complete control, we ask that You forgive us for things we have said, thought, done...for everything that has been unpleasing to You...

We want our hearts to be right before we place our petitions before You.

In Your Word You told us to cast our burdens on You, because You care for us...

We believe You right now…Lord, we ask *not* that You take the storm out of our lives because we know that all things work for the good of those who love You and are called unto Your purpose. We love You, Lord. We ask that You be with us and help us through the storm and give us the wisdom that once we get out of the storm, we have the holy boldness necessary to tell a dying world that Jesus is Lord! Father we do not want to be like the Israelites and keep going around the mountain and questioning Your love and dedication to us. We trust You!

Thank You, God for sending us in the fire, through the fire, and to the other side where peace resides.

Let the words of my mouth, the words of this book, and the meditation of my heart be acceptable to you – My Lord and My Redeemer.

This is a picture of my husband (Eric and I) in 2018.

My husband and our son

Eric, Bria, and Haley

When my babies were really babies....

This picture includes my three heartbeats, Haley, Eric, and Bria (in 2021). This picture was taken after he returned to college. They visited him for a couple of days.

If you or someone you know need Transformational
Life Coaching, please complete the contact page on my webpage
www.IAmDrBridgette.com

I will get in touch with you to set up a free discovery call.

QR Code To My Website: